SO-ABA-853

Life in the American Colonies

The Scoop on CLOTHES, HOMES, and DAILY LIFE in Colonial America

REVISED EDITION

by Elizabeth Raum

Consultant:
Dr. Samuel B. Hoff
Professor of History
Delaware State University
Dover, Delaware

CAPSTONE PRESS
a capstone imprint

Fact Finders is published by Capstone Press,
1710 Roe Crest Drive, North Mankato, Minnesota 56003.
www.capstonepub.com

Copyright © 2012, 2017 by Capstone Press, a Capstone imprint.
All rights reserved.
No part of this publication may be reproduced in whole or in part, or stored in a retrieval system,
or transmitted in any form or by any means, electronic, mechanical, photocopying, recording,
or otherwise, without written permission of the publisher.
For information regarding permission, write to Capstone Press,
1710 Roe Crest Drive, North Mankato, Minnesota 56003.

Library of Congress Cataloging-in-Publication Data is available on the Library of Congress website.
ISBN 978-1-5157-9746-3 (paperback)
ISBN 978-1-5157-9380-9 (ebook)

Editorial Credits
Mandy Robbins, editor; Ashlee Suker, designer; Wanda Winch, media researcher;
Eric Manske, production specialist

Photo Credits
Alamy Stock Photo: Hilda DeSanctis, middle right 17, PARIS PIERCE, 16; Bridgeman Images:
Massachusetts Historical Society, Boston, MA, USA/James Brown Marston, 28, Sneden, Robert Knox
(1832-1918)/Virginia Historical Society, Richmond, Virginia, USA, 27; Capstone Press, (floral) design
element throughout, (rocking chair) design element throughout; Capstone Studio: Karon Dubke, inset
17; Getty Images: Hulton Archive, 8, MPI, 10, Stock Montage, 12; Granger, NYC: Sarin Images, top
19; North Wind Picture Archives, Cover, 7, 15, 20, 22, 25, 26; Shutterstock: alexkar08, (burlap) design
element throughout, Anastasia Litvinenko, bottom right 14, eAlisa, 23, Irina Tischenko, (board) design
element throughout, Kadroff, bottom 19, Mona Makela, 11, Nigel Paul Monckton, left 14, photocell,
(fram) design element throughout, Piotr Malczyk, top 21, STILLFX, 24, Viachaslau Kraskouski, (floor)
design element throughout, Vladyslav Danilin, bottom 21

Printed in the United States   4316

TABLE OF CONTENTS

Introduction   Many Cultures, One Land 4

Chapter 1   Getting Dressed 6

Chapter 2   Choosing a Home 12

Chapter 3   Working to Live 18

Chapter 4   Fun and Games 22

Chapter 5   On the Move 26

Glossary 30

Read More 31

Internet Sites 31

Index 32

Primary Source Bibliography 32

Many Cultures, One Land

The people of colonial America were a strange mix. Colonists came from many countries, including England, the Netherlands, Germany, Sweden, and France. Their customs varied as much as their languages. Some colonists came seeking adventure. Others, like those at Jamestown, Virginia, hoped to get rich through trade. The Pilgrims who settled in Plymouth, Massachusetts, wanted religious freedom.

In America, colonists also met American Indians. Dozens of tribes lived on America's east coast. Each tribe was unique. The Iroquois were as different from the Algonquins as the English were from the Swedes.

In 1619 the first Africans arrived in America. These people didn't come by choice. Slave traders forced them into slavery. Their numbers increased slowly. By 1675 about 5,000 Africans lived in the colonies.

custom—a tradition in a culture or society

4

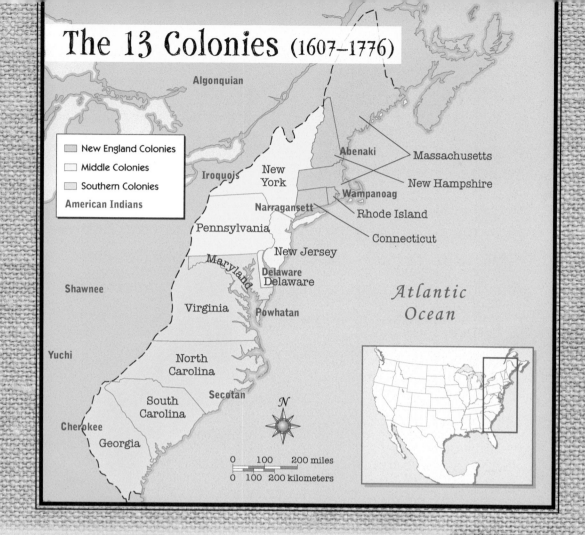

The 13 Colonies (1607–1776)

Algonquian

Legend:
- New England Colonies
- Middle Colonies
- Southern Colonies
- American Indians

Abenaki — Massachusetts
— New Hampshire
Iroquois
New York
Wampanoag
Narragansett — Rhode Island
Pennsylvania — Connecticut
New Jersey
Maryland
Delaware
Delaware

Shawnee

Virginia   Powhatan

Atlantic Ocean

Yuchi

North Carolina

Secotan

South Carolina

Cherokee
Georgia

N

0   100   200 miles
0   100 200 kilometers

Throughout the colonial period (1607–1776), European colonists, American Indians, and African slaves learned from one another. They exchanged ideas to create homes, clothing, and customs. This sharing of ideas resulted in a culture that became uniquely American.

Fast Fact

Not all slaves came from Africa. European slave traders also brought slaves from the Caribbean Islands.

Chapter 1

Getting DRESSED

You could tell a lot about colonists from the clothes they wore. Farmers and laborers wore loose clothing made of cheap fabric so they could work comfortably. So did servants and housewives. Wealthy people wore fine fabrics designed to impress others. Their clothes were too fancy and too tight for work.

Clothing styles varied from colony to colony. In the hot south, people wore lightweight cotton or linen clothes. In chilly New England and the cooler Middle Colonies, people wore warm wool.

UNDERWEAR

A colonist's outfit began with underwear. But underwear wasn't what you might expect. All colonial men wore long-sleeved white undershirts that reached their knees. Women and children wore shifts instead of shirts. A shift was a long-sleeved dress that fell below the knees. No one bothered with boxers or briefs. Underpants weren't common in America until the 1830s.

STAYS

Women and children wore stays over their shifts. A stay was made of stiff pieces of whalebone, reeds, metal, or wood. They were sewn into a tight-fitting garment that went from waist to chest. Stays forced women and children to stand straight. They also made it hard to bend over or play. Many boys wore stays until age 6. Girls wore them all their lives. They even wore stays at night when sleeping.

Fast Fact

In colonial America, fancy clothes were known as dress clothes. Everyday work clothes were called undress.

Colonists wore their very best clothes to church.

WOMEN AND CHILDREN GET DRESSED

Over their stays, girls and women wore several light skirts called petticoats. Over the petticoats a woman would wear a gown and an apron. Women's gowns had long sleeves and skirts. Colonists considered elbows and ankles ugly, so they kept them covered. Women also wore neck cloths and caps.

Wealthy women wore fancy hoop skirts. Hoops gave these dresses a rounded shape. But they weren't very practical. Hoop skirts made it impossible for women to sit down!

Babies and young children wore simple dresses. That's right, even boys wore dresses. At about age 6, boys were "breeched." This custom meant they could finally ditch the dresses for knee-length pants called breeches.

No matter the weather, colonists dressed in several layers of clothes.

Fast Fact

Colonial shoemakers made children's shoes at least two sizes too big. Children wrapped their feet in thick, itchy wool until they grew into the shoes.

Anna Green Winslow, age 12 (written in 1772)

"I was dressed in my yellow coat, my black bib and apron, my [high-heeled] shoes, a cap with blue ribbons on it, and a very pretty locket in the shape of a heart. I wore my new cloak and bonnet, gloves, and so on."

MEN GET DRESSED

All men wore breeches. But what they put on next depended on their jobs. A farmer would wear a sleeveless vest and a jacket. The jacket protected clothing from animals and dirt. Rich men strutted about in fancy coats made of brightly colored silk.

In the 1700s, it was also fashionable for wealthy men to wear wigs. Wigs were heavy, hot, and expensive. They were made of human, horse, or goat hair. The hair was tied with colored ribbons. Boys from wealthy families began wearing wigs when they were breeched.

The first colonists were shocked by how little clothing American Indians wore.

BUCKSKIN LEGGINGS AND BUFFALO ROBES

While colonists were sweating in layers of clothes, American Indians went nearly naked. Their style was based on comfort and usefulness in daily life.

Women wore skirts or dresses made of buckskin or mulberry bark. Most men wore breechcloths. Eventually, some American Indian men adopted European styles. They wore hats, shirts, and blankets that they received from European fur traders.

In winter both men and women added buckskin leggings for warmth. Buffalo, beaver, bear, or rabbit robes kept them cozy on cold days.

buckskin—a strong soft material made from the skin of a deer

breechcloth—a piece of deerskin clothing that hangs from the waist and passes between the legs

NOT-SO-FANCY FOOTWEAR

When it came to footwear, some native people went barefoot. Walking barefoot during childhood built up tough calluses on their feet. Calluses protected them from the pain of walking on pebbles, sticks, and prickly plants.

Other American Indians wore moccasins. These soft leather shoes were often attached with a strap around the ankle. Moccasins were comfortable to wear and protected feet from rough ground.

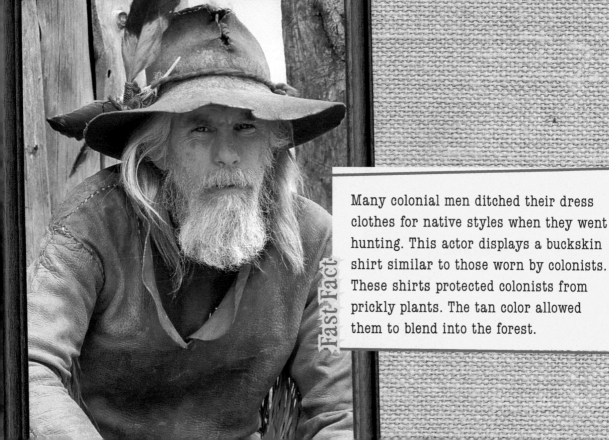

Fast Fact

Many colonial men ditched their dress clothes for native styles when they went hunting. This actor displays a buckskin shirt similar to those worn by colonists. These shirts protected colonists from prickly plants. The tan color allowed them to blend into the forest.

Chapter 2

Choosing a Home

The Iroquois surrounded their villages with protective walls called palisades.

When the colonists arrived, there were already villages in America. But these homes belonged to American Indians.

In the cold northeast, Abenaki and Wampanoag people lived in wigwams. These small houses had arched roofs and wooden frames covered with bark. They were cozy in winter and cool in summer. Many Eastern Woodland Indians built longhouses. Up to 60 people lived in each wooden longhouse. People hung woven mats or wood screens to separate rooms. The Algonquian tribes of the Middle and Southern colonies used wigwams and longhouses. Both could be built in a few days, and they could last 10 years or more.

FIRST COLONIAL HOMES

Some early colonists took over abandoned wigwams. Others tried to build their own. But English wigwams were not warm or weatherproof like Indian wigwams. The English structure had a door in one end and a fireplace in the other.

Some settlers dug cellars 6 or 7 feet (1.8 or 2.1 meters) into the ground for homes. Only the thatched roof showed above the ground. These houses were damp, dark, and dirty. The earth helped keep colonists warm. But it also allowed bugs, mice, and snakes to skitter and slither in.

Fast Fact

Storms and fires were a constant danger. Strong winds could knock down simple houses. Straw roofs caught fire.

thatched—made of woven straw

13

After the first few years, colonists built houses of logs, bricks, or stones. Brick was a great choice because it was durable and colonists could make it themselves. Brickmakers made bricks by combining water, clay, and sand and baking them over a hot fire.

An early colonial home was usually about 20 by 20 feet (6 by 6 m) in size. The walls were thin and had many cracks. The door was so small that visitors had to crouch to enter. There were no windows, so houses were dark. A fireplace provided a little heat and lots of smoke. Soot covered everything.

Fast Fact

At night the only light came from the fireplace or candles. Most people used tallow candles made of animal fat. The candles smelled like rotten bacon.

A visitor to a New Jersey home in 1679 wrote:

"The house was so poorly built that if you are not so close to the fire as to almost burn yourself, you cannot keep warm, for the wind blows through everywhere."

[Text has been changed for clarity.]

Most houses had one main room, called a hall, where everyone gathered, ate, and slept. Sometimes there was a loft over the main room where children slept. A lucky family owned a table and one chair. At night, they put mattresses stuffed with straw, grass, or cornhusks on the floor as beds.

Colonial fireplaces were used for warmth, light, and for cooking.

MANSIONS AND PLANTATIONS

By the 1700s, New England merchants had built brick or stone mansions with many rooms and fine furniture. Houses were still cold because there was no insulation. Wind seeped through the walls and roofs. To combat this chilly problem, every room had a fireplace.

In the Middle and Southern colonies, the problem was not cold wind, but heat. Wealthy farmers lived on plantations. Plantation houses also had many rooms and fine furniture. High ceilings kept rooms cool in the hot, muggy climate. Large windows let in light and air. The kitchen was in a separate building to keep cooking odors and heat away from the main house.

Fast Fact Thomas Jefferson's Monticello and George Washington's Mount Vernon were colonial plantations.

Many plantation homes had tall columns around the main entrance.

SLAVE HUTS

Slaves cleaned, cooked, and polished furniture in elegant plantation houses. But they slept in simple huts with dirt floors. Some slave huts were made of bricks or wood. Others were African-style round huts with thatched roofs. But thatched roofs leaked. African huts didn't last long in the South's wet winter weather.

Bathrooms?

Imagine you traveled back in time and asked a colonist where the bathroom was. They would probably hand you a pot or point you to an outdoor shed. You see, no one—rich or poor—had indoor bathrooms.

People used an outdoor toilet with a pit dug beneath it for waste to drop into. Anyone who couldn't go outside used a chamber pot. When the pot was full, colonists sometimes dumped it out the window. There was no soft toilet paper either. Colonists often wiped their bottoms with corncobs!

There were two toilet options in colonial times—the pit or the pot.

insulation—a material that stops heat, sound, or cold from entering or escaping

plantation—a large farm in the southern colonies

Chapter 3

Working to LIVE

Colonists didn't have any of the modern conveniences that we have today. Nothing came easy. They worked hard just to survive.

WOMEN'S WORK

Keeping up a colonial home was a woman's main job. Women and girls cared for children, prepared and preserved food, and worked in the gardens. They knitted, mended clothes, made candles, and did laundry.

Colonial housework often required heavy lifting. Doing laundry meant hauling heavy pails of water to the house. Women boiled the water over a smoky fire and scrubbed filthy clothes by hand. They laid clothes on rocks or bushes to dry. In New England, it was nearly impossible to do laundry in the winter. People wore dirty, smelly clothes until the weather improved.

When the Pilgrims first landed in America, they did laundry on the shore.

Doing laundry required soap, but colonists couldn't buy it at a store. They had to make it. Making soap was a messy job. First, women and girls soaked ashes in water to make lye. Then they purified stinky cooking fat by boiling it over an outdoor fire. When they mixed the fat with lye it became soap.

lye—a strong substance used in making soap and detergents

MEN'S WORK

Men and boys worked long hours outside the home. Whatever the job, they usually ended up very sweaty and dirty. Farmers cleared land, planted crops, cut trees, and built homes. They tended animals and put up fences.

Farmers did their work with simple tools.

Men also worked at different trades. Millers worked at mills grinding grain into flour. Carpenters built homes, barns, and other buildings. Blacksmiths fashioned metal into useful items like tools, pots, and cooking utensils. There were also basket makers, cabinetmakers, shoemakers, and many more tradesmen.

Boys were expected to help with work from a young age. Farm boys chopped firewood, fed animals, and mended fences. By the time they were teens, many boys became apprentices to tradesmen. They worked with the goal of becoming tradesmen some day.

trade—a particular job or craft, especially one that requires working with the hands

apprentice—someone who learns a trade or craft by working with a skilled person

Chapter 4

FUN and GAMES

COMMUNITY CELEBRATIONS

American colonists were busy, but they still found time to celebrate. Births, weddings, and even funerals provided reasons for people to get together. Adults found ways to make work fun too. They got together for quilting bees and barn raisings. Colonists also held harvest festivals and celebrated New Year's Day.

Dancing was a fun part of many colonial wedding celebrations.

In the Southern colonies, people traveled great distances to go to plantation parties. The owners held dinner parties, dances, and hunts. Parties might include horse racing, card playing, and a fancy dress ball. Slave musicians often supplied the music for plantation dance parties. Guests sometimes stayed for several days.

Fast Fact

In Virginia it was against the law to hunt, fish, or play games on Sunday. Everyone was expected to be in church.

Pinkster

Each spring during the 1700s, slaves from New York to Maryland celebrated Pinkster. It began as a Dutch tradition during a religious holiday called Pentecost. Dutch people gave their slaves time off to visit family on that day.

Soon African-Americans adopted the holiday as their own. They gathered in towns and cities to visit, play games, and dance. Many people sold items such as berries, herbs, and oysters at Pinkster markets.

AMERICAN INDIAN GAMES

American Indians valued celebrations too. Many tribes held footraces, swimming races, and other contests.

In the winter, the Iroquois played the snow snake game. Men competed to see who could throw a stick shaped like a snake the farthest.

American Indians also enjoyed ball games. Several tribes played a game that involved kicking a leather ball against a post. It was almost like football.

Child's Play

When their chores were done, colonial children found time to play. Boys made boats to float in streams. Girls played with dolls often made out of corncobs, sticks, or fabric. All children played with tops, puzzles, marbles, and balls.

Many colonial games are still played today. Hide-and-seek, hopscotch, and tag were favorites. Children also sang "London Bridge" and "Ring Around the Rosy."

American Indians had played lacrosse for hundreds of years before white people ever knew about the game.

In the southeast, Cherokee, Choctaw, and Creek boys played lacrosse. Each person used two sticks to pass a deerskin ball back and forth. In the northeast, Iroquois used a single long stick to play the game. Lacrosse is still popular today throughout the United States and Canada.

Newspaper Notice from
Boston Gazette, May 22–29, 1721:

"There will be a Pig Run for Boys, at 9 in the morning. The Boy who takes the Pig and fairly holds it by the Tail, wins the Prize."

Chapter 5

On the MOVE

Before there were any roads, waterways provided the best travel routes.

Colonists took travel tips from the American Indians. American Indians had found ways to make travel easier in the American wilderness. They had created well-worn foot paths over hundreds of years. American Indians used light canoes to travel easily over waterways. They also had tricks for making travel easier in the winter. Snowshoes made it possible for people to walk on thick snow without sinking. Toboggans were useful for hauling supplies over snowy land.

Wagon wheels carved deep ruts in colonial dirt roads.

For the colonists, walking was faster than riding horses. Healthy men and women could walk about 40 miles (64 kilometers) in 10 hours. The first horses were brought to the colonies from England in 1609. They were smaller than today's horses and needed to rest often. Traveling by horse-drawn carriage or wagon didn't work well anyway. The first colonial roads were made of dirt. They were narrow and full of ruts. There weren't any bridges, either. Travelers had to find ways around rivers and streams or wade across them.

Fast Fact

In the 1750s, the New York colony had only 57 miles (92 km) of roads. These dirt trails were just wide enough for one wagon.

snowshoe—a racket-shaped frame for walking on snow
toboggan—a long, flat sled that curves up at one end

GROWING AND CHANGING

Over time, colonists improved the roadways and bred stronger, larger horses. But even on better roads, carriages and wagons bounced over bumps and got stuck in mud. Travelers arrived at journey's end tired, dirty, and shaken up.

By the end of the colonial period, Boston, Massachusetts, was a bustling city.

A Complaint Written in 1778:

"The main road has become so bad, as to greatly delay travelers. Trees have fallen across it and are not removed; the roots are not cut up; a number of crossings are swampy and full of holes; and many of the bridges are nearly impassable."

[Text has been changed for clarity.]

During the colonial period, American Indians and colonists struggled to live together peacefully. American Indians taught colonists many skills that helped them survive. But as more colonists arrived from Europe, land became scarce. American Indians were pushed west.

By the mid-1700s, the colonists had built a foundation for the future. People lived in warm, sturdy houses. There was plenty of food thanks to farmers, fishermen, and hunters. There were stores, schools, and libraries. Life had changed in many ways, but even bigger changes were coming. Frustration with British rule was growing. After fighting the Revolutionary War (1775–1783), the colonies would be colonies no longer. They would become the United States of America.

bred—when humans have purposely mated animals to produce offspring with desired qualities

GLOSSARY

apprentice (uh-PREN-tuhs)—someone who learns a trade or craft by working with a skilled person

bred (BRED)—when humans have purposely mated animals to produce offspring with desired qualities

breechcloth (BREECH-kloth)—a piece of deerskin clothing that hangs from the waist and passes between the legs

buckskin (BUHK-skin)—the skin of a deer

custom (KUHS-tuhm)—a tradition in a culture or society

insulation (in-suh-LAY-shun)—a material that stops heat, sound, or cold from entering or escaping

lye (LYE)—a strong substance used in making soap

plantation (plan-TAY-shuhn)—a large farm; before 1865, plantations were run by slave labor

snowshoe (SNOH-shoo)—a frame used for walking on snow

thatched (thach)—made of woven straw

toboggan (tuh-BOG-uhn)—a long sled that curves up at one end

trade (TRADE)—a particular job or craft, especially one that requires working with the hands

READ MORE

Kalman, Bobbie. *A Visual Dictionary of a Colonial Community.* Crabtree Visual Dictionaries. New York: Crabtree Pub. Co, 2008.

Mara, Wil. *The Innkeeper.* Colonial People. New York: Marshall Cavendish Benchmark, 2010.

Raum, Elizabeth. *The Dreadful, Smelly Colonies: The Disgusting Details about Life During Colonial America.* Disgusting History. Mankato, Minn.: Capstone Press, 2010.

INTERNET SITES

FactHound offers a safe, fun way to find Internet sites related to this book. All of the sites on FactHound have been researched by our staff.

Here's all you do:

Visit *www.facthound.com*

Type in this code: 9781429661386

Super-cool stuff!

Check out projects, games and lots more at
www.capstonekids.com

INDEX

African–Americans, 4, 5, 17, 23
American Indians, 4, 5, 10–11, 12, 24–25, 26, 29

bathrooms, 17

celebrations, 22–23, 24
clothing, 5, 6, 18–19
    breechcloths, 10
    breeches, 8, 9
    children's clothing, 6, 7, 8, 9
    men's clothing, 6, 9, 11
    shoes, 9, 11
    stays, 7, 8
    underwear, 6
    women's clothing, 6, 7, 8

farming, 6, 9, 20, 21, 29
furniture, 15, 16
games, 23, 24, 25
    lacrosse, 25

homes, 5, 12–17, 18, 29
    longhouses, 12
    mansions, 16
    plantations, 16, 17, 23
    slave huts, 17
    wigwams, 12, 13
housework, 18–19
    laundry, 18–19
    soap making, 19

Jefferson, Thomas, 16

Pinkster, 23

toys, 24
trades, 21
traveling, 26–29
    bridges, 27, 29
    canoes, 26
    horses, 27, 28
    roads, 27, 28, 29

Washington, George, 16
wigs, 9

PRIMARY SOURCE BIBLIOGRAPHY

Page 9—based on the writings of Anna Green Winslow in the *Diary of Anna Green Winslow,* originally published in 1984 by Houghton and Mifflin of Boston.

Page 15—based on an anonymous observer's quotation as published in *The Colonial Experience* by David Freeman Hawke (Indianapolis: Bobbs-Merrill, 1966).

Page 25—as published in the *Boston Gazette,* May, 1971.

Page 29—based on an observer's quotation as published in *Colonial America,* by Oscar Theodore Barck, Jr. & Hugh Talmage Lefler (New York: The Macmillan Company; London: Collier-Macmillan; second edition, 1968).